Accounting

Accounting Made Simple for Beginners, Basic Accounting Principles and How to Do Your Own Bookkeeping

Table of Contents

Introduction 1

Chapter 1: What is Accounting 2

Chapter 2: Basic Principles of Accounting 12

Chapter 3: Accounting Concepts 15

Chapter 4: Introduction to the Accounting Equation 22

Chapter 5: The Financial Statements 25

Chapter 6: Preparing an Income Statement 28

Chapter 7: Statement of Owner's Equity 33

Chapter 8: Reading the Balance Sheet 36

Chapter 9: Reading the Cash Flow Statement 40

Chapter 10: Depreciation 44

Chapter 11: Financial Ratios 47

Chapter 12: Inventory Accounting 53

Chapter 13: Taxes and Accounting 55

Chapter 14: Definitions of Accounting Terms 57

Conclusion 61

Introduction

Thank you for taking the time to pick up this book about accounting. Throughout the following chapters, you will be taken step by step through the accounting process, and will gain a fundamental understanding of key accounting principles.

This book aims to educate the reader on basic accounting practices, primarily those relating to small businesses. You will soon learn about the accounting equation, the different financial statements, financial ratios, taxation, and much more.

If you're not a numbers person, don't worry. This book aims to simplify the accounting process, and provide the reader with a good understanding of how accounting works – regardless of their prior experience.

Once again, thanks for choosing this book. I hope that the information contained in the following chapters allows you to better understand, manage, and grow your business. Best of luck!

Chapter 1: What is Accounting

Accounting is known as the language of business. The information we collect from accounting allows us to have a better understanding of our own business, as well as to provide stakeholders in our business a greater understanding of its performance. Accounting is the voice of your business and through your efforts in accounting, you are able to talk back to your business to meet goals, objectives, and fulfil values.

If you were to take a business owner who had invested $100,000 of his own money to start a small office supply business, how would he be able to understand how much his business is making and how well his initial investment is performing? Accounting is the answer.

We could take a look at the figures, how much of the $100,000 we have left and see that we might have used around 30% of those funds. From that we can determine we have spent around $30,000 once the business had established to buy the initial equipment and inventory to get things off the ground. We would then have $70,000 of the investment left to continue working on the business. If we were to have made around $50,000 in profit from sales of office equipment, we would determine that we would have around $120,000 in our cash accounts.

This is a simple explanation of how accounting is used. There is far more information that can be collected and analyzed through accounting such as the income made through the business, how much debt is owed on the business, and how healthy the investment is. We are able to learn all this and more through accounting.

What Does Accounting Mean?

We can't go much further without having a definition of what exactly accounting is. Fortunately, it is a requirement for accounting bodies to provide a technical definition, and while these vary from institution to institution, they all come down to very similar concepts. For the purpose of this book we will use the American Institute of Certified Public Accountants (AICPA) definition which is as follows:

"the art of recording, classifying, and summarizing in a significant manner and in terms of money, transactions and events which are, in part at least of financial character, and interpreting the results thereof."

There are many unofficial definitions which we can cover to allow you to have a greater understand of what accounting is outside of the more technical definitions.

Accounting can be considered an art form due to the fact that we use skills and creative judgment in order to approach the discipline and perform the functions well. We can also consider accounting as a science as it is a body of knowledge, however it would fall more into the category of social science as the rules and principles are constantly shifting and improving as accounting develops and adapts to the changing world of business.

There are many interconnected phases of accounting which all come together in harmony for us to present and understand the information. Recording works to write down and keep records of all transactions the business carries out. Classifying comes down to grouping items which have been recorded and comprise of similar characteristics. The classified information is then summarized into reports which are easily digested, and these reports are known as financial statements.

Accounting involves transactions and events that are concerned with financial character. There are other transactions and interactions that businesses conduct that are not of financial character and these are not recorded in our financial statements. This means anything with a financial value is expressed through account such as salaries, acquisition of office equipment, and sales of goods.

Interpreting the results as part of the accounting process means taking the information that we have compiled during the previous accounting phases and creating documents that are easy to understand, interpret, and use to improve the business. The information we collect such as amounts, figures, and other data are not much good on their own. From there, we are able to use that information to make decisions in our business and determine the direction we are going to take in the future. Without this type of information it would be like flying a plane with our eyes closed and not looking at what the instruments are telling us. While that may be dangerous up in the air, it can be dangerous in a business sense to be not using any of the data our business is telling us.

There are many activities that we do day to day which can fall under the category of accounting, both in business and everyday lives. This could be something as simple as having a monthly budget, checking receipts from the supermarket each week to determine how much we are spending and where, as well as just keeping track of how much we earn and what we will be spending that money on. Just like in our everyday life, if we were to just spend money wherever we please, we would find that it is quite difficult to make important financial decisions.

The Purpose of Accounting

Now that we have a basic understanding of what accounting is, we can learn a little more about what we can use this information for and how it affects our decision making in business. The purpose of accounting is to provide information from an economic entity, which can be a profit or non-profit business, to users who require that information to make economic decisions. Who are these decision makers? They are more than just the owner of the business and depending on the structure of the business, which we will explore in later chapter, there can be a number of decision makers such as:

Management

Investors

Creditors

Lenders

Government

Employees

Customers

Others

The information is generally used to determine the entity's profitability, stability of operations, ability to pay obligations, tax bases, as well as other information. Let's break it down into how each statement affects these decisions. We will take a look further into each of these items in more detail a little further in the book, but for now we will just bring these to your attention.

1.   Results of operations - This gives some insight into the performance of the company over certain period of time. This could be a year, a quarter, or even just a month. You can calculate the results of the operation by deducting the expenses incurred from the income earned. This will give you the figure of net income.

2.   Financial Position - This will give an idea of what resources the business has available to it in comparison to what the business owes to third parties. You will also see what remains for the owners after all debts have been paid. This statement is divided into three classes. These are Total Assets on one side and the liabilities along with the capital in the second and third categories.

3.   Solvency and liquidity - This determines how secure the business is when it comes to the debts outstanding. Solvency is

what measures the businesses ability to pay the debts as they are due, whereas liquidity is the business's short-term ability to pay debts.

4.   Cash Flows - These statements detail when cash flows into the business and flows out of the business as the business goes through its day to day activities.

5.   Other Statements - We can source further information from other financial statements that provide information of qualitative, quantitative, and financial nature. Any information that have a determining factor in the decision making of users is generally found in the financial reports.

Users of Financial Statements

Now that we understand how this information is used, let's take a look at who are the users making decisions with the information found in the financial statements. Each user has a different perspective of the statements and a variety of different decisions to make using the information provided to them.

Owners and Investors

In larger organizations, the owners are considered the stockholders of the information. These are people who have invested their money to help run the business, and they want to make sure they know how their investment is performing. They would have the options to hold their stocks, sell, or invest more if the business is performing well. In the small business sense, the owners are those who run the business themselves. They need this information to determine the next steps for their business, so they can either continue doing what they are doing, pivot and improve, or close up shop.

Management

Management can either be the owners in the case of small businesses, or they can be professionals who are trained in the operation of a business in all aspects such as finances, employees, inventory, sales, and more. These managers are essentially acting as agents of the owners.

The managers are tasked with making many economic decisions at all levels, this being true of the owners and hired managers. They must also use this information to report back to their superiors whether that be higher level managers and executives, or the owners of the corporation or business. These could be related to questions such as how much inventory and supplies the business will need to order, how much cash the business has to spend, whether the business is meeting targets, and other questions which will affect the course of action.

Lenders

Lending money to a business carries risk and for this reason the lenders, whether they are banks or financial institutions, will want some insight into whether or not the business will be able to pay back their liabilities when the time comes.

Government

The authorities and governing bodies will show an interest in the businesses performance for taxation and regulatory reasons. Taxes are determined by the results of the businesses operations with many factors to consider. The government will therefore take a look into the financial statements when tax time comes around.

Employees

As an employee, you would want to know the performance of the company you work for when it comes to profitability and stability. This can allow employees to determine how stable their job is, and whether their own salaries are in line with how the business is performing, as well as whether there is any opportunity to further their career as the company expands.

Customers

Depending on the type of business, customers may also have a vested interest in the performance of a business. This is particularly true for B2B businesses that might have an ongoing long-term contact with the company, where the customers rely on the business to continue operations for their own supply chain. This would be true of a supplier and reseller which have an agreement. If the reseller was to discover that their supplier is becoming insolvent, they would need to make the decision to start looking for new suppliers.

Types and Forms of Business

We know that the basic definition of a business entity is an organization that takes economic resources in order to provide goods and services for their customers in exchange for money. We can break these businesses down into three distinct categories or types of business, of which they can take of three forms once broken down further.

Service Business

These types of businesses provide products without physical form which are known as intangible products. These are generally in the form of skill on behalf of the service provider which can translate to expertise, advice, or something else of value to the customer. Some examples are repair shops, hair salons, banks, accounting firms, and consultancies.

Merchandising Business

These businesses are those that sell products to consumers after purchasing products from suppliers or wholesalers. These businesses specialize in buying and selling with their profit coming from the products they sell being sold at a higher price than what they had been purchased at. We interact with these businesses virtually every day with some examples being grocery stores, convenience stores, and distributors.

Manufacturing Business

Differing from a merchandising business, a manufacturing business purchases raw materials, and uses them to create an entirely new product. These products are then delivered to other customers who are generally businesses, such as the merchandising businesses to be sold onto retail customers. An example of a manufacturing business would be a car manufacturer or a furniture builder.

Hybrid Business

Not all businesses are clearly defined in these categories with some taking on aspects of one or more. This could be considered for the case of a restaurant which uses ingredients to create a meal. This would fall under the category of manufacturer, as well as selling products such as wine which would be considered merchandising, but also providing a service to the customer by fulfilling their orders. These types of businesses generally fall under their own class.

Forms of Business Organizations

Businesses come in a few primary forms based on their ownership. These are:

Sole Proprietorship

These are generally small business which are owned by a single person. They are the easiest to set up and also the cheapest to run compared to the other options. The owner and the business are considered one entity which means the owner has unlimited liability, and their debts and the business's debts are one and the same. This means that creditors can collect on the assets of the owner, should his business become illiquid. An example of a sole proprietor would be a food stall at the local market, or a freelancer working with clients. These businesses don't have too many assets typically, nor do they take on a great deal of liabilities, meaning they are generally self-funded and are more likely not to take risks which could damage their business.

Partnership

Similar to a sole proprietorship, the partnership is comprised of two or more people, investing their resources to build the business. These partners then share the profits amongst them at an agreed upon percentage. There can be two types of partnerships, these being general and limited. General works the same as a sole proprietorship in that the partners have unlimited liability, whereas in a limited partnership, creditors may only collect on assets belonging to the business and not the partners. Partnerships operate the business in a similar way to the sole proprietorship, however rather than being owned and funded by just one person, they are owned by two or more.

Corporation

The corporation is considered to be an entity of its own, which is legally separate from those that own the business and have invested their money. This allows the owners who are known as stockholders to have limited liability when it comes to creditors collecting on the debts of the business. However, the stockholders also have limited control in the decisions made by the business. Instead, the stockholders are able to elect a group of people to form a board of directors which make the decisions regarding the company such as electing a CEO to lead the business. This is not the case for all corporations, with some being owned by a small number of people with varying shares in the business. Corporations can be public, in that they are owned by members of the public with shares sold on the stock exchange, or private with shares being exchanged by selected people who are either outside investors or hold a position in the corporation.

Limited Liability Company

In the USA, there is another form of business which takes features from both corporations and partnerships. These businesses are not incorporated in the same way that a corporation would be, however they are still able to provide benefits to the owners by limited their liability in a similar manner. An even greater advantage is that LLC's are able to decide how they would be taxed, whether it be as a sole proprietorship, partnership, or corporation.

Cooperative

This is another form of business that is created by a group of individuals, known as members, for some kind of mutual benefit. These types of businesses can be either incorporated or unincorporated. An example of a cooperative would be companies that provide utilities such as water and electricity, or banking such as credit unions.

Chapter 2: Basic Principles of Accounting

Now that we have a solid understanding of what accounting is, how it works, who uses the information and how businesses are operated, we can look further into the basic principles of accounting and how we can create the financial statements. These basic principles are important to understand, as they can help readers of financial statements to avoid any misconceptions which could cloud judgment and dilute the information. These principles dictate how we prepare financial statements and can be thought of as guidelines for how to approach certain situations.

Assumption of Going Concern

The assumption of going concern simply means that it is assumed that the business will be operating indefinitely or at least in the near future. What this means in reality is that financial statements are put together with the understanding that the business will continue to operate for as long as the statements project, with no reason to assume that anything will change. This helps put together balance sheets which assume that assets are valued at the price that was paid for them, rather than what they would be sold at today. Similarly, long term assets are assumed to be used until no longer possible, with their value remaining the same.

Accrual Basis of Accounting

Using the accrual method means that the revenue or income that we collect is only recognized when earned, regardless of when we receive the income, and similarly, expenses are only recorded as they happen rather than when they are paid.

Using this method, we have different expenses for when cash is collected and when it is paid out. This means that we would record both income and expenses when they have been realized, despite the fact they may never be paid or if there is a delay. This means that we could have an income recorded in mid-December despite the fact it may not be paid until early January. This allows us to place the information in the correct categories and avoid any information doubling up or being misreported. There is also Cash Accounting which is when transactions are recorded as the cash moves from one account to another. Some small business owners and sole traders may opt for the cash account method as this is more compatible with how they do business. In larger corporations, the accrual method of accounting is the most widely used.

Time Period (Periodicity)

There is an assumption that while the business may be unlimited in its lifetime, we still need to divide this lifetime into time periods. This is known as the periodicity assumption. Each of these time periods are divided into equal amounts and help us prepare the financial reports on the financial position and performance of the business over these time periods. This helps us find more meaning in the information we have collected. The time periods which are generally used are across 12 month periods using either a calendar year or fiscal year.

You are probably aware of the difference between the two, with a calendar year being the period beginning January 1st, travelling through the 12 months until December 31st. A fiscal year on the other hand is across 12 months throughout any date on the calendar. For example, a business could select for this to be from April 1st until March 31st or July 1st to June 30th.

Accounting Entity Assumption

This assumption is based around how we identify the business for the purpose of accounting. Regardless of the structure of the business, we will always recognize it as separate and distinct from those who own and manage the business as well as the employees that hold the business together. This means that all personnel transactions on behalf of the owners, managers, and employees that are not part of the business will not be recorded in the accounting process. There are some items that are often a grey area with owners charging them as a business expense despite them being primarily for personal use. This can cause trouble further down the line if audited by the IRS, so if in doubt it is always best to check with a reputable accountant.

Monetary Unit Assumption

There are two characteristics for the monetary unit assumption. These are the quantifiability, and stability, of the currency. For the records to be quantifiable, all records will need to be stated in terms of money which are generally in the currency of the country the business exists in, or where the records are being prepared. The stability of the currency, which can be in dollars, euros, pounds, pesos or any other currency, is the assumption that the currency will remain stable in its purchasing power and that inflation will not affect the currency over the course of the time period.

Chapter 3: Accounting Concepts

Accounting can be broken down into three major elements which each play a role in the information we publish in our financial statements. These major elements are: Assets, Liabilities, and Capital. We will take a look at each of these elements further before going into detail on how to read, interpret, and compile our own financial statements.

Understanding Your Account

Before we get started learning about the elements of accounting, we first need to understand the meaning behind the word "account". Your account is a type of storage unit where information is collected and stored. An example would be your cash account. This is where all your transactions are stored with all cash receipts and payments. For each of the payments and deductions, there will be a record made under the cash account. The same can be said for all other accounts such as a building account, IT account, and inventory account. These accounts will interact with each other as transactions are made from one account to another, such as the cash account to the IT account.

Assets

Assets are the lifeblood of the business. These are the resources which the business has control over through ownership as a result of their past transactions. Assets provide economic benefits into the future, and improve the cash flow of the entity. Assets can be in the form of properties or rights owned by the business, and are broken down further into two classifications: current, and non-current.

Current Assets

The assets that are considered current are those that are held within a short period of time, up to 12 months, before they are consumed. Cash is considered a current asset as it is moves frequently from one account to another over a short period of time. To gain a greater understanding of what can be known as a current asset, here are some examples:

1.   Cash and Cash Equivalents - This is comprised of bills and coins as well as cash stored in the bank or checks that still need to be transferred.

2.   Receivables - These are funds that are owed to you from customers, also known as accounts receivables as well as notes receivable which are receivables supported by notes promising the receiving of the funds at a date in the foreseeable future. These can also be rents receivable for those businesses that hold assets generating rental revenue. Interest is another form of receivable. In this category, there may also be an allowance for doubtful accounts. This is a separate account that can be used to deduct from the asset an amount that is set aside with the assumption that there will be some accounts that will simply not be received for whatever reason. This enables the business to still operate despite accounts that may go unpaid.

3.   Inventories - These are assets that are prepared to be sold for the purpose of generating revenue for the business.

4.   Prepaid expenses - These are expenses that the business has paid in advance. This could be the case for rent, insurance, advertising, and office supplies.

Non-Current Assets

These are assets that are not exchanged or transferred frequently. They are expected to be held for the long term over a period longer than 12 months, or for however long the company plans to operate. Below are some examples of non-current assets:

1.   Long-term Investments - These are investments which are held over the long term to fulfil the objectives of the business. They could be in the form of stocks, bonds, and real estate.

2.   Land - These are lands which the business operates on. They are not to be sold unless the business was to move operations.

3.   Building - These are the buildings located upon the land in which the business operates. They could be an office, factory, warehouse, or storage facility.

4.   Equipment - These are the things that fill those buildings. Equipment can be in the form of furniture, machinery, and fixtures such as shelves, tables, chairs as well as office equipment, computer supplies, and more. Equipment can have an accumulated depreciation that can be applied to determine the value as the asset slowly wears out over time and becomes obsolete. This is known as a contra asset that deducts a certain amount over time of the assets total value.

5.   Intangibles - These are assets which are not physical but still add value to the business. They can be in the form of goodwill, patents, copyrights, and trademarks that are owned by the business.

Liabilities

The liabilities are the obligations required of the business which require payment. A business can source an asset from two major sources which determine whether the source is considered a liability or a form of capital. These are borrowing money from lenders or credits or if they owner was to invest their own funds into the business. Therefore, liabilities are considered to be claims by parties' other than the owners against the assets held by the company. Similar to how we classify assets in current and non-current, we do the same for liabilities.

Current Liabilities

1. Trade and other payables - These are items that the business needs to pay such as accounts payable, notes payable, interest payable on borrowings, and accrued expenses.

2. Current Provisions - These are short term liabilities that can be easily measured.

3. Short Term Borrowings - These are small loans, financing arrangements, and credit arrangements that are used to supplement cash flow in a short-term sense.

4. Current portion of a long-term liability - This is when payables are due. They may be a smaller portion of a long term borrow that is due, and the business must pay it using the current account.

5. Current Tax Liability - These are paid when the business has taxation due for the period.

Non-Current Liabilities

These are liabilities which are not due anytime within the next 12 months. This means that company needs not pay what is due within the period measured. These include:

1. Long-term notes, bonds, and mortgages which are paid over the long term.

2. Tax liabilities which have been deferred.

3. Other long-term obligations.

Capital

As we mentioned before, capital is used to purchase assets alongside liability. This is also known as the owner's equity or net assets, and is essentially what is left over after all the liabilities have been settled. The equation is therefore capital equals total assets minus total liabilities. Capital can be in the form of investment on behalf of an owner in the case of smaller businesses, or it could be financing from the sale of shares to stockholders in a corporation. Capital can fluctuate based on:

1. Contributions by the owners in the form of investments.

2. Withdrawals made by owners such as dividends or owner's salary.

3. Income.

4. Expenses.

As the owner contributes their own investment into the business or if the business was earning an income, capital increases. Whereas if the owner wanted to pay himself or in the case of the company, offered dividends, capital will decrease. In the case of a business that is owned by a single person or a sole proprietorship the capital is known as the Owner's Equity, whereas partnerships call this Partners Equity. Corporations, as they are owned by stockholders, call this account Stockholder's Equity.

Income

In addition to the three elements of accounting, we also need to take a look at both income and expenses. Income provides economic benefits for the business over the course of the accounting period by increasing assets or decreasing liabilities and as a result, increases the overall equity aside from the contribution of the owners.

Income is comprised of both revenue and gains. Revenues are tied into what the business earns during its operations. This could be professional fees, service revenue in the case the business offers services, or sales if the business is engaged in merchandising or manufacturing.

Gains can come from activities such as the selling of other assets such as equipment, short term investments, and other assets.

Income is recorded throughout every period and is part of the capital account. There are a number of income accounts, each with their own purpose such as service revenue, professional fees, rental income, commissions, income on interests, royalties, and basic sales accounts.

Expenses

Expenses have the opposite effect of income, in that they decrease the economic benefits of the business over the course of the accounting period, meaning they decrease the value of assets while increasing the liabilities, causing a decrease in equity.

Expenses are comprised of ordinary expenses that are incurred over the course of the business operating day to day such as Cost of Sales, Advertising Expenses, Rental Expenses, Salaries and Wages, Income Tax, Repairs, and losses that can occur from time to time such as fire damage, water damage, or theft. Expenses are measured much the same as income in that they are measured over the course of the accounting period and then closed as a part of capital.

Net Income is calculated as total income minus total expenses.

Chapter 4: Introduction to the Accounting Equation

As mentioned in the previous chapter, accounting relies on a basic equation in order to keep the books balanced. This provides an indication that everything has been accounted for and recorded in the operation of the business. The equation is as follows:

Assets = Liabilities + Capital

We know that when a business purchases resources or assets, they are comprised of two sources. That is either the contributions from an owner in the form of capital, or borrowed money from creditors or lenders in the form a liability. This means that assets can only come from these two sources, making the equation possible.

We also know that in the operation of the business, the transactions which take place move figures and information from one account to another, or one category such as from liabilities to assets meaning that regardless of what happens in the business, the equation will remain balanced. This means that every transaction has a double effect. With every transaction, at least two accounts are affected.

In order to understand a little better, we can use the following example:

Mr. Thompson wants to start a business manufacturing candy. In order to start the business, he needs $50,000. Having only $20,000 of his own money, he borrows the remaining $30,000 in the form of a loan from the bank, while investing the $20,000 of his own money. With a balance of $50,000 he then purchases $1,000 worth of machinery.

Transaction	Assets	=	Liabilities	+	Capital
1. Owner's investment	20,000.00	=	-	+	20,000.00

We can see from this first transaction that the capital Mr. Thompson put into the business translated to assets in the form of cash. This also increased the capital the owner has in the business by the same amount. This was before he had sourced the loan from the bank so for now, liabilities remain at zero.

Transaction	Assets	=	Liabilities	+	Capital
1. Owner's investment	20,000.00	=	-	+	20,000.00
2. Loan from bank	30,000.00	=	30,000.00	+	-

As we can see here, once he had obtained a loan from the bank, the assets once again increased as a result of the additional cash funneled into the business. However, since this cash still technically belongs to the bank in the form of the obligation to repay, we have it listed in the liabilities column. Notice that we are still able to balance the equation with these two transactions.

Transaction	Assets	=	Liabilities	+	Capital
1. Owner's investment	20,000.00	=	-	+	20,000.00
2. Loan from bank	30,000.00	=	30,000.00	+	-
3. Purchased printers	1,000.00 (1,000.00)	=	-	+	-

Once Mr. Thompson purchased the machine, we experienced a decrease in assets. However, since the machinery itself is an asset, we also gained $1,000 in assets, and therefore there is no difference in total assets although there is a decrease in the cash account, and an increase in another, the equipment account.

If we were to use the formula now, we can see that Mr. Thompson's books have been balanced. If we take the liabilities of $30,000 and add the capital of $20,000 we come to the figure of $50,000 of assets.

Chapter 5: The Financial Statements

Now that we have an understanding of the basics behind accounting and the equation that brings it all together, it is time to discuss the financial statements. This is where you are able to see the information displayed in an easily digestible format, and can better interpret the information in order to make decisions. The complete set of financial statements include 5 components which we will be exploring in this chapter, before we move deeper into each of the financial statements.

Statement of Comprehensive Income

The Income Statement also goes by the name Profit and Loss Statement, or P&L. This shows the operations of the business over the course of the time analyzed. This allows those reading the statement to have an understanding of the businesses income and expenses, as well as how much it has made or lost over the course of this time.

This is an essential document for many businesses both small and large. Some larger companies and those that want a more in-depth analysis will prepare a Statement of Comprehensive Income. This provides income on the company's results in its operations as well as other comprehensive income or OCI. The other comprehensive income takes into account the gains and losses that are not commonly found on the Income Statement, which could be from revaluation surplus, translation adjustment, or unrealized gains. If a company has no other comprehensive income, then the Income Statement and Statement of Comprehensive Income would be no different.

Statement of Changes in Capital

The Statement of Changes in Capital is how we are able to record the capital account over the course of a period of time. We start with the initial balance and record all the changes before recording the end balance. There are a number of ways in which capital can be affected, such as through contributions and withdrawals by the owner as well as income and expenses. The statement goes by different names depending on the form of ownership of the business. For example, in the case of a sole proprietorship, the document would be called the Statement of Owner's Equity. In the case of partnership, it is known as Statement of Partners' Equity, and for corporations, it is known as the Statement of Stockholders Equity.

Statement of Financial Position

This is also known as the balance sheet and displays the assets, liabilities, and capital of the business at a given point in time. This shows the business' financial position and health, and rather than being presented over the course of a period of time, it is taken on a specific date, which is recorded at the top of the statement. As mentioned in the previous chapter, the assets should equal the total amount of both the liabilities and capital.

Statement of Cash Flows

This is known as the cash flow statement and it shows the changes in balance of cash over the course of a period of time, ultimately displaying the cash balance at the end of the period. The cash flow statement displays the inflows and outflows from the business' day to day operations in investing, financing, and operating.

What we mean when we say operating is the activities that are a direct result of the company's main course of business. Investing is when the business places funds into assets or long-term investments such as the purchasing of real estate, plant, and equipment, as well as other non-current activities. Financing is where the business carries out transactions in order to raise funds whether that be from the bank in the form of a loan or a contribution from the owners or shareholders for the purchase of assets. Any time cash flows in or out of the business for whatever reason, it will be recorded on this statement.

The Interconnectedness of the Financial Statements

A relationship exists between each of the financial statements with interrelated information. For this reason, the financial statements are generally prepared in the order presented above to ensure that the available information has been prepared before the next financial statement is being put together. We do this because some information will need to be taken directly from one statement in order to complete another. We will be able to see this in practice when we take a look at each financial statement on its own, and see how certain figures are borrowed from statements prepared prior. Some examples of these are relationships are:

1. Net income calculated and presented in the Income Statement is used when we prepare the Statement of Changes in Equity as the net income and expenses has an effect on the capital.

2. When we come to the ending balance of Capital in the Statement of Owner's Equity, it is then transferred over to the balance sheet under Capital.

3. In determining the cash balance in the Balance Sheet, we use this for the Statement of Cash Flows. Once we have our ending balance in terms of cash in the Statement of Cash Flows, we then place that figure into the Balance Sheet.

4. We also have notes in our financial statements which show supporting computations of the amounts, and additional information about what we have presented in the above reports.

Chapter 6: Preparing an Income Statement

We now know that the Income Statement is also known as the Profit & Loss or P&L Statement, and this is a breakdown of the results of the businesses operations over a period of time. Using the revenues and expenses of the business we are able to compute the net income or net loss.

An Example of the Income Statement

To get a better understanding of how the Income Statement works, it is best to look over an example. In this case we are taking a look at a sole proprietorship business, going back our example of Mr. Thompson and his candy manufacturing business. Keep in mind that these amounts are only for illustration purposes and have been simplified for our example. They do not represent any existing business.

Thompson Candy Co.

Income Statement

For the Year Ended December 31, 2016

Sales Revenue	$ 160,000
Less: Expenses	
Salaries Expense	$ 40,000
Supplies Expense	26,100
Rent Expense	20,500

Utilities Expense	11,300	
Depreciation Expense	5,000	102,900
Net Income		$ 57,100

From here we can run through what these figures mean. We know that the income statement displays the net income or net loss of a business. To calculate this, we simply deduct all the expenses from the income to come to our net figure which in this case is $57,100 in net income.

An income statement generally starts with the heading consisting of three lines. The first is to let the reader know which company they are looking into, and as such we place the company number right at the top of the page. Secondly, we have the title of the report so we know which statement is being read. Finally, the third heading mentions the period being covered in the report to avoid any confusion.

You will notice that the third title mentions "For the Year Ended…" the reason for this is that the income statement covers the information over a specific timespan. In the case of example above, we are looking over the 12 months prior to December 31, 2016 starting January 1st of that year. This means we need to know when this period ends in case we are confused by statements that might be using a different period of time, such as a fiscal year.

We take down all the income accounts before moving onto expenses. As you can see the income from the business is sales revenue. As a manufacturer, there are few ways that the business is able to earn other income, with a majority of the income coming from the sale of products to distributors.

We then take down the expenses following the income accounts. It is generally good practice to arrange expenses accounting to amount, taking down largest to smallest. This helps you determine where expenses are coming from in terms of their size, and by arranging them in this way you are able to have a greater understanding of the expenses, and can keep reports more organized. Despite having this order, we generally take Miscellaneous Expense or Sundry Expense last as this is often the least important, unless it is abnormally large in which case, the large expenses in this category should have an account of their own.

In the case that income is greater than expenses, we have a net income. If expenses are ultimately greater than income, then we have a net loss. We present these calculations using a single line which is drawn following every amount. When we have reached our final computation, we use a double ruled line to signal that we have finished our calculations. For our example, this is $57,100 of net income.

You will also notice that the income statement is consistent with the accrual basis of accounting which we explored in an earlier chapter. As a reminder, this is when income is recognized upon when it is earned rather than when it is collected. This is the same as expenses which are recorded when they are incurred, regardless of when they are paid. This means that our income statement displays those incomes and expenses that have been earned and incurred, respectively despite the fact they may not have been collected or paid.

Statement of Comprehensive Income

We also explored in the previous chapter, the Statement of Comprehensive Income. This is generally added into the financial statements as per International accounting standards' suggestions. These are often added to the end of the income statement as a similar but separate list of "other comprehensive income". The other comprehensive income records gains and losses that are separate from profit and loss. These could be unrealized gains and losses, as well as revaluation surpluses that add income to the business outside of the normal business operations.

In the case that the company does not have any comprehensive income as a part of its operations, the Income Statement and Statement of Comprehensive Income will be the same. We would still use the title Statement of Comprehensive Income, in accordance with International Accounting Standards, regardless.

Below is an example of a Statement of Comprehensive income which has some accounts relating to other comprehensive income. This is generally for more complex business operations rather than small business owners who prepare their own financial statements and accounting.

Thompson Candy Co..

Statement of Comprehensive Income

For the Year Ended December 31, 2016

Service Revenue		$ 160,000
Less: Expenses		
Salaries Expense	$ 40,000	
Supplies Expense	26,100	
Rent Expense	20,500	
Utilities Expense	11,300	
Depreciation Expense	5,000	102,900
Net Income		$ 57,100
Net Income		$ 57,100

Other Comprehensive Income

Revaluation Surplus	$ 20,000	
Unrealized Translation Gain	10,200	30,200
Total Comprehensive Income		$ 87,300

Chapter 7: Statement of Owner's Equity

Once we have prepared our Income Statement, the next step is to prepare the Statement of Owner's Equity or the Statement of Changes in Owner's Equity. Throughout this chapter, we will demonstrate what the Statement of Owner's Equity looks like, and how we make changes to it.

As mentioned earlier in the book, the Statement of Owner's Equity records the changes made in the capital account whenever there are contributions and withdrawals from the owner, as well any net income or loss that occurs as a result of business operations. We know that capital is increased as the owner invests income through contributions, as well as by income made from profits in the business. On the other hand, withdrawals in the form of payments to the owner, dividends, as well as expenses or losses, remove capital from the business.

Example of a Statement of Owner's Equity

In the case of a sole proprietorship, the statement of owner's equity will show the movement of capital depending on four factors. Using the example below, we can see that the company started at the beginning of 2016 with $100,000 in capital. Over the course of the business, the owner invested in a further $10,000 as well as withdrew $20,000. In this case, the Statement of Owner's Equity will look as below.

Thompson Candy Co.

Statement of Owner's Equity

For the Year Ended December 31, 2016

Thompson, Capital	$ 100,000
Add: Additional Contributions	10,000
Net Income	57,100
Total	$ 167,100
Less: Thompson, Drawings	20,000
Thompson, Capital – Dec. 31, 2016	$ 147,100

Similar to the Income Statement, the Statement of Owner's Equity will also consist of a three-line heading with the name of the company being first, the title coming second, and third being the period covered.

Depending on the form of business we are analyzing, the statement will be known by different names. For example, in the case of partnerships, the title we would use would be the "Statement of Partner's Equity" and for corporations, we would call it the "Statement of Stockholders' Equity"

Also, similar to the Income Statement, we measure the Statement of Owner's equity over a specific span of time. For this example, we look over the period of January 1st, 2016 to December 31st, 2016.

We are also able to see from this example, how our income and expenses affect capital. By calculating our net income (income minus expenses) we are able to arrive at the figure that would be added to our capital account. If expenses were to exceed income, we would experience a net loss, decreasing your capital account.

You will also notice that the net income figure is the same as what we had in the Income Statement, since this is where we collect this figure and also the reason why the income statement will need to be completed first.

We can see the that the owner had withdrawn $20,000 over the course of the year which is reflected in the decrease of the capital balance. We are also able to see that the company finished the year with $147,100 in capital, starting with the $100,000 invested in the beginning of the year, the $10,000 in contributions over the year, as well as the $57,100 in net income while deducting the $20,000 in withdrawals.

Once we have finalized our balance for the year through these calculations, we then use the double ruled line to signal that this is the final figure that has been computed, being the $147,100.

Chapter 8: Reading the Balance Sheet

Once we have established the owners' equity, we can move onto preparing the next financial statement, the Balance Sheet. You may remember from earlier in the book that the balance sheet shows the financial position or condition of a business, at a certain date rather than over the course of a specific period of time. What we mean by the financial position is that we want to take a look at all the resources belonging to the business, as well as the claims against them in the form of liabilities and capital.

Balance Sheet Example

Using the same business for our example, below is the Balance Sheet for Thompson Candy Co. Keep in mind that these amounts have been simplified for the teaching purposes of the example, and that an official balance sheet will usually look much more in depth.

Thompson Candy Co.

Statement of Financial Position

As of December 31, 2016

ASSETS

Current Assets:

Cash	$ 21,000		
Accounts Receivable	16,000		
Prepaid Expenses	4,500	$	41,500

Non-current Assets:

Property, Plant and Equipment	145,000
Total Assets	$ 186,500

LIABILITIES AND OWNER'S EQUITY

Current Liabilities:

Accounts Payable	$ 8,400		
Rent Payable	8,000	$	16,400

Non-current Liability:

Loans Payable	23,000
Strauss, Capital	147,100
Total Liabilities and Owner's Equity	$ 186,500

As the balance sheet shows the financial position and condition of the company, it may also be known by the name "Statement of Financial Position". Similar to both our Income Statement and Statement of Owner's Equity, we start the statement of with the three lines of the company name, the title of the report and the date of the report.

You will notice that the date of the report is different from our previous two, and is worded "As of..." rather than "For the Year Ended...". This is because we present the information of the balance sheet as of a certain date, taking a snapshot at a specific point in time. Since we are preparing our financial documents at the end of the year in this example, we take the date of December 31st, 2016 similar to our previous two. However, the balance sheet can be prepared anytime of the year, whenever the reader wants to know the financial position of the company.

The balance sheet takes account of all the assets, liabilities, and capital within the company. As mentioned previously, the assets can be anything the company owns such as the buildings, cash, machinery, and equipment etc. Liabilities are the obligations the business has to the creditors and lenders, meaning part of those assets may be claimed by creditors in order to settle any debts. The capital on the other hand is what the owner himself has claim to through their contributions to, and their earnings from, the business.

We classify the assets and liabilities into current and non-current to determine the frequency in which they will change. We know that the current assets are those that can be converted into cash within 12 months, or are simply cash itself. Current liabilities are those which are obligations that are due within 12 months, and could be bills and invoices that are to be paid up soon, rather than non-current liabilities such as a mortgage or loan. The accounting equation ensures that total assets will always equal total liabilities and capital, which determines who has a claim to what in the business.

You will notice that we had also used the $147,100 from the Statement of Owner's Equity to determine the Owner's capital. Again, this is why we prepare all financial statements in order to have all fields accounted for. If we were to do the balance sheet first, we would be missing the owners' equity and would not be able to complete a balanced equation for the total assets.

There are two ways in which we are able to present the balance sheet. These are in the account form, and the report form. In the account form, we would present the assets on the left side while the liabilities and capital are both presented on the right similar to a ledger. The report form is the one we used for this example in which we presented assets first, and then liabilities and capital below.

Similar to how we prepared our last two statements, we would use a single line for each amount computed, before using a double ruled line for the totals of assets, liabilities, and capital.

Chapter 9: Reading the Cash Flow Statement

The cash flow statement allows the reader to have an understanding of the movement of cash as a result of the operations of the business. We are able to see both the inflows and outflows of cash whenever the business earns income through receipts, or incurs expenses through payments. We categorize these activities into three classes - operating, investing, and financing.

While accounts are generally concerned with the accrual basis when it comes to measuring the income and expenses of a business, it is still important to see the movement of cash over a period of time to determine how well the business is able to receive and pay out cash.

Statement of Cash Flows Example

Using our same example for Thompson Candy Co. once again, we are able to see how the business manages cash, and where this cash moves to and from over the course of the year.

Thompson Candy Co.

Statement of Cash Flows

For the Year Ended December 31, 2016

Cash Flow from Operating Activities:

Cash received from customers $ 146,000

Cash paid for expenses	(81,000)	
Cash paid to suppliers	(47,500)	$ 17,500

Cash Flow from Investing Activities:

Cash paid to acquire additional equipment	(20,300)

Cash Flow from Financing Activities:

Cash received from investment of owner	$ 10,000	
Cash received from bank loan	50,000	
Cash paid for bank loan – partial payment	(27,000)	
Cash paid to owner – withdrawal	(20,000)	13,000
Net Increase (Decrease) in Cash for the Year		$ 10,200
Add: Cash – January 1, 2016		10,800
Cash – December 31, 2016		$ 21,000

We can see here that all the inflows and outflows for all the different activities of the business have been recorded. Following these movements, we are presented with a balance at the end of the statement which shows how much money we have left in the account for the new year. We know that the cash inflows are in the form of receipts or payments from customers, while the outflows are payments by the business, or are disbursements.

Once again, we use the three headings at the top of the statement, the name, the title of the report, and the period covered. For the cash flow, we would obviously want to record the movements over a specific period of time to determine how healthy the business was in its movements of cash. If we were to have cash flow issues over this time, it would mean that further financing may be required by the business.

You will notice that each of the inflows and outflows are classified within the three activities being operating, investing, and financing. This is to help understand where cash is moving within the business.

Operating activities are those that are concerned with the main operations of the business. These can involve the rendering of professionals' services, acquisition of inventory and supplies, selling of those inventories through merchandising or manufacturing, the collections of accounts, payment of accounts when dealing with suppliers, as well as other activities. These generally affect the current accounts of both assets and liabilities.

The transactions which are classified as investing are those where the business places money for long term purposes. This involves the purchasing of real estate as well as plant, and equipment. Investing can also involve the investment of long term securities. When the business sells the investments or properties it has purchased, this would also be classified under investment. A good way to think of investing is the transactions that involve non-current assets.

The transactions that fall under financing activities can be associated with where the business gets its funds. This involves transactions where the owner invests further money into the business, or if the business was to receive a bank loan or some other form of long term payables with creditors. When the business repays these liabilities through withdrawal by the owner, or payment of loans to banks or creditors, we would also classify these transactions as financing. Financing is generally concerned with the non-current liabilities and capital.

To avoid any confusion, we present all the figures in the balance sheet in positive figures, while the outflows are negative and in parentheses, to calculate them simply. Once we have all the inflows and outflows presented, we calculate the net increase or decrease in cash which is then added to the balance we started with to bring us to the balance at the end. This allows us to have the cash balance at the beginning of the period, see the changes throughout the period, and how this affected the balance at the end of the period.

You will also notice that the cash balance at the end of the period is the same as we had in the cash account in our balance sheet. We would do the Statement of Cash Flows prior to the balance sheet since it is calculated over the course of the year, whereas the balance sheet is at a certain point in time.

Chapter 10: Depreciation

Under the GAAP (Generally Accepted Accounting Principles), there are several methods of depreciation that may be used. Depreciation is where you can claim the devaluation of assets over time, against the amount of tax that your business owes.

The official GAAP definition of depreciation is as follows:

'Depreciation is a systematic and rational process of distributing the cost of tangible assets over the life of assets.'

Depreciation Methods Based on Time

Straight Line Method

This method of calculating depreciation is done as follows:

Depreciation = (Cost – Residual Value) / Useful Life

Example: On April 1, 2011, a company purchased equipment at a value of $140,000. This equipment is estimated to have a useful life of 5 years. At the end of the 5th year, the salvage value (residual value) will be $20,000. The company recognizes depreciation to the nearest whole month.

Depreciation value for 2011 = ($140,000 - $20,000) x 1/5 x 9/12 = $18,000

Depreciation value for 2012 therefore = ($140,000 - $20,000) x 1/5 x 12/12 = $24,000

Declining Balance Depreciation Method

Using this method, you calculate the depreciation as follows:

Depreciation = Book Value x Depreciation Rate

Book Value = Cost – Accumulated Depreciation

Example: Using the same example as above, and assuming the equipment once again has a useful life of 5 years with a residual value of $20,000, the company chooses to recognize depreciation to the nearest month.

Depreciation for 2011 = $140,000 x 40% x 9/12 = $42,000

Depreciation for 2012 = ($140,000 - $42,000) x 40% x 12/12 = $39,200

Sum of the Year's Digits Depreciation Method

Here, where 'n' represents the number of years of useful life, depreciation is calculated as follows:

Depreciation Expense = (Cost – Salvage Value) x Fraction

Fraction for the first year = n / (1+2+3+...+n)

Fraction for the second year = (n-1) / (1+2+3+...+n)

Fraction for the third year = (n-2) / (1+2+3+...+n)

...

Fraction for the last year = 1 / (1+2+3+...+n)

Example: A company purchased an asset on January 1, 2011. The acquisition cost of the asset is $100,000 and the useful life of the asset is 5 years. The residual value of the asset at the end of useful life is $10,000.

Depreciation expense for 2011 = ($100,000 - $10,000) x 5/15 = $30,000

Depreciation expense for 2012 = ($100,000 - $10,000) x 4/15 = $24,000

Which Method to Use

The straight line method of calculating depreciation is the most commonly used method. It charges an equal amount of depreciation to each accounting period, and is the simplest to calculate. Though, the choice of which method you use is largely up to you. Your choice should depend upon which method is most suitable for your business, and the assets which you are calculating it for.

Chapter 11: Financial Ratios

We use financial statements to measure various functions of the business and to gain further information on how the business is performing. Calculating financial ratios is a method of analysis whereby we take two items in our financial statements and compare the two, with a resulting figure that provides further insight. Throughout this chapter, we will be taking a look at the various financial ratios, how they can be calculated, and what this means for the business. The financial ratios can be classified by what they measure such as profitability, liquidity, management efficiency, leverage, as well as valuation, and growth.

The financial ratios can be expressed as a percentage which is calculated by multiplying the decimal number by 100.

Profitability Ratios

Gross Profit Rate = Gross Profit ÷ Net Sales
This ratio is one of the most basic. It calculates how much gross profit is earned by the business from its sales. The gross profit is equal to net sales, this being sales minus sales returns, discounts and allowance, and subtracting the cost of those sales.

Return on Sales = Net Income ÷ Net Sales
This is also known as the net profit margin or net profit rate. It is a measure of the income as a percentage of sales. The higher the Return on Sales is, the more profitable the business will be.

Return on Assets = Net Income ÷ Average Total Assets
This is a measure of the return on investment to evaluate how efficiently the business is being managed. By determining the return on assets, we are able to see how well the business is using the assets and resources available. The higher the number, the better the business is performing with its assets.

Return on Stockholder's Equity = Net Income ÷ Average Stockholder's Equity
This ratio measures the percentage of income derived from every dollar of owners' equity. It helps determine how much each stockholder is making on their dollar, and how well their investment is performing.

Liquidity Ratios

Current Ratio = Current Assets ÷ Current Liabilities
This ratio helps us evaluate the ability for a capital to pay its short-term obligations such as bills, loan repayments, and other current liabilities using available assets such as cash, current receivables, inventory, and any prepayments that have been made.

Acid Test Ratio = Quick ÷ Current Liabilities
The acid test ratio is also known as the quick ratio as it measures the ability for business to pay the short-term obligations such as bills, loan repayments, and utilities using liquid assets such as cash, marketable securities, and current receivables rather than all current assets as with the current ratio.

Net Working Capital = Current Assets - Current Liabilities
This measures whether a business is able to meet its current obligations with current assets, as well as seeing what is left over, or if the business is faced with a deficit.

Cash Ratio = (Cash + Marketable Securities) ÷ Current Liabilities
This is a measurement of the businesses' ability to pay its current liabilities using just cash and marketable securities. This is to determine how liquid a business is, rather than how soluble it is.

Management Efficiency Ratios

Receivable Turnover = Net Credit Sales ÷ Average Accounts Receivable

This is a measure of how efficient the business is when it comes to extending credit and collecting the same. The number which is calculated will present the number of times in a year the company collects any open accounts. The higher the number, the more efficient the business is in the credit and collection process, indicating that is safer and more secure to lend to.

Days Sales Outstanding = 360 Days ÷ Receivable Turnover
Also known as "receivable turnover in days or the collection period. The ratio measures the average number of days it would take the business to collect an outstanding receivable. The lower the number, the faster the business is able to collect receipts.

Inventory Turnover = Cost of Sales ÷ Average Inventory
This ratio is an indication of how many times inventory is sold to customers and replenished. You may like to use sales rather than cost of sales which is a matter of preference. The higher the ratio, the more frequently inventory is sold and more efficiently managed.

Days Inventory Outstanding = 360 Days ÷ Inventory Turnover
This allows us to view the inventory turnover in days. The number represents how long inventory is sitting in storage. The figure is an indication of how many days from purchase to sale of a piece of inventory. You would ideally want to keep the DIO as short as possible as this means you are moving inventory at a much greater rate.

Accounts Payable Turnover = Net Credit Purchases ÷ Avg. Accounts Payable
This figure represents how many times a business is paying the accounts payable over the course of a given time period. Having a low ratio in this case is ideal as it would mean the business is able to delay payments for a longer period of time, while using the money for more productive, income producing purposes before paying obligations.

Days Payable Outstanding = 360 Days ÷ Accounts Payable Turnover

This ratio indicates the average number of days before the business is paying its obligations to suppliers. It could also be called for simplicity purposes, accounts payable turnover in days. You could also call this the payment period. It would be ideal to have this figure be as long as possible as the business having liquid money in the accounts for more productive purposes is of greater importance than paying current liabilities faster.

Operating Cycle = Days Inventory Outstanding + Days Sales Outstanding
This figure is a measurement of the number of days the business is able to make 1 complete operating cycle. In other words, this would be how long it would take the business to purchase merchandise, make a sale, and collect the receipts due. The smaller the period the better, as the business would be able to generate sales and collect the receivables much faster.

Cash Conversion Cycle = Operating Cycle + Days Sales Outstanding
This is a measurement of how fast the business is able to convert cash into further cash. Essentially this is how many days the business takes to pay for purchases, sell them, and collect the receipts. Ideally, this would be as short as possible as it shows how fast the business is able get a return on their purchases.

Total Asset Turnover = Net Sales ÷ Average Total Assets
This is a measurement of the overall efficiency of a business in how they are able to generate sales with the assets available. This is quite similar to the ROA, however we are using net sales rather than net income, taking an efficiency approach rather than profitability.

Leverage Ratios

Debt Ratio = Total Liabilities ÷ Total Assets
This is a measure of how much a business' assets are financed by debts. We would ideally want this to be as low as possible as it means the business has less obligations to third parties, with owners having more equity in the business' assets.

Equity Ratio = Total Equity ÷ Total Assets
This ratio is similar to the debt ratio in that it determines the portion of total assets that are financed by equity, the owner's contributions to the business, as well as the business funding itself through profits.

Debt Equity Ratio = Total Liabilities ÷ Total Equity
This is an evaluation of the capital structure of the business. Having the ratio of more than 1 indicates that the business is a leverage firm, whereas having a ratio below one would indicate that the business is a conservative one.

Times Interest Earned = EBIT ÷ Interest Expense
This is a measurement of how often the interest expense is converted to income and whether the business is able to pay its interest expense using profits earned. The EBIT is pure earnings before interest and taxes are deducted.

Valuation and Growth Rates

Earnings per Share = (Net Income - Preferred Dividends) ÷ Average Common Shares Outstanding
The earnings per share shows the rate earned per share of common stock. The preferred dividends are then deducted from net income to arrive at the figure of earnings available to the common stockholder.

Price-Earnings Ratio = Market Price per Share ÷ Earnings per Share
This ratio is used when we want to determine whether a stock is over or under priced. The lower the ratio the more likely it is that the company is underpriced. Investors are attracted to lower price earnings ratios as it can indicate the growth rate of the stock will be much greater.

Dividend Payout Ratio = Dividend per Share ÷ Earnings per Share
This ratio determine how much of the net income is being distributed to the owners. In larger companies, income is shared

amongst the owners as well as a significant portion kept for the business to carry on through to the next year.

Dividend Yield Ratio = Dividend per Share ÷ Market Price per Share
This ratio is a measurement of the percentage returned through dividends when taking a look at the price paid for the stock. The higher the yield, the more appealing it will be to investors who are seeking higher dividends rather than long term growth through capital appreciation.

Book Value per Share = Common SHE ÷ Average Common Shares
This ratio is an indication of the value of the stock when taking a look at its historical cost. We would then look at the value of common shareholder's equity across a period of time and then divide this by the average common shares outstanding.

Chapter 12: Inventory Accounting

Accounting for inventory can be a difficult thing to do, and there are several different methods for doing so.

The most commonly used accounting systems are the perpetual inventory system, and the periodic inventory system.

Perpetual

The perpetual system requires that accounting records show the amount of inventory on hand at all times. It holds a separate account in the subsidiary ledger for each good in stock, and is updated any time the inventory levels change.

Determining the COGS (cost of goods sold) requires taking inventory. The most common methods of valuating the inventory under a perpetual system are:

- First in, first out (FIFO)

- Last in, first out (LIFO)

- Highest in, first out (HIFO)

- Average Cost

These methods all produce different results because they are based upon differing assumptions.

With the FIFO method, you are basing the cost flow on the chronological order in which purchases are made. With LIFO on the other hand, you are basing the cost flow in a reverse chronological order. The average cost method produces a cost flow based on the average cost of goods.

The important thing here is to simply stick with one method of recording your inventory.

Periodic

In the periodic system, sales are recorded at the time they occur, but the inventory is not updated. A physical inventory count must be taken at the end of year to determine the cost of goods for that period.

Which Method to Choose?

The choice of which inventory management system you use (if you require one) is up to you. There are however, a few key differences to be aware of before making your decision.

To record purchases using the periodic system, you will debit the Purchases Account. Conversely, doing the same using the perpetual system you will debit the Merchandise Inventory account.

To record sales, the perpetual system requires an entry to debit the COGS and another to credit the Merchandise Inventory. By recording the COGS for each sale, the perpetual system alleviates the need for adjusting entries and calculating COGS at the end of a financial period, which can be a big time-saver.

Chapter 13: Taxes and Accounting

The decision of whether you do your taxes yourself when it comes to that time of the year or have someone handle them for you is a challenge for many small business owners. The decision you make can be dependent on the size of your business, how good you are with the numbers, as well as your own personal preferences. There are pros and cons to hiring when it comes to tax time and we will be exploring those in this chapter.

Size of the Business

The definition of small business can vary depending on who you are asking or what form you are filling out. With taxation, there is no rule that says if your business is this size, that you must employ a taxation professional. The smaller the business, the more likely and worthwhile it may be to do your taxes yourself. Your business size is generally measured by how many employees you have. For example, if you have under 10 employees there is far less work involved in doing your own taxes, whereas anything over that number might become a little difficult, and it that case it would be best to send the work to an accounting professional.

How Much Time Do You Have?

Small business owners are generally well invested in their business. This means time can be constrained and doing your own taxes may be the least of your priorities. You may have a number of employees that you able to delegate tasks to which can help free up some of your time, but not everyone has this advantage. If you have some time set aside when it is tax time, then you may like to go ahead and do your own taxes. If it affects the rest of your schedule, you could be better off outsourcing.

Opportunity Cost

Going on from the last point, even if you are able to free up some time, it is time well spent? You may have some other tasks or assignments that are a better use of that time rather than doing your own taxes. Similarly, on the other side of the coin, you may have better uses for the money spent in hiring a taxation professional. For example, you could invest those funds in growing your business. You will need to assess what it will cost you for each option and make a decision from there. There is no right or wrong answer in this case since this situation will be unique to your business.

Knowing the Math

Not everyone is able to work well with numbers. Most small business owners have a bit of experience with numbers but this doesn't mean they enjoy it or are any good at it. Having to do this kind of work can stress some people out, confuse them, or cause them to have a mental breakdown. There are also those who work extremely well with numbers, it all makes sense to them and they find it incredibly easy. In this case, you would make a decision whether to do your own taxes or not based on how well you are able to calculate and compute many of the elements we have explained throughout this book.

Knowledge of Taxation Law

Tax law can change rapidly and if you are not up to date with the latest in legislation then you might find it difficult to work through your own taxes. Fortunately, there are professionals who are some of the first to know in regard to changes to tax law and by hiring out your taxation work, you are able to ensure that no mistakes are made. You might enjoy however, the research side of things and staying up to date with any changes in which case you may find it more satisfying and worthwhile to do your own tax accounting. In short, there is no correct answer here, and the choice is up to you.

Chapter 14: Definitions of Accounting Terms

Accounting can be over-complicated at times by different acronyms and terms. This chapter is dedicated to defining the most common accounting terms that you'll come across.

Accounts Receivable (AR)

The amount of money owed by your customers after goods or services have been delivered.

Accounts Payable (AP)

The amount of money you owe creditors in return for the goods or services that they have delivered.

Current Assets (CA)

Current assets are assets that will be used within one year. Typically, this will include cash, inventory, and accounts receivable.

Fixed Assets (FA)

Fixed assets are assets that are long-term, and will likely provide benefits to a company for more than one year. Examples are a building, land, or machinery.

Balance Sheet (BS)

A financial report that summarizes a company's assets, liabilities, and owner's equity at a given time.

Capital (CAP)

A financial asset and its value, such as cash or goods. Working capital is calculated by subtracting current liabilities from current assets.

Cash Flow (CF)

The revenue or expense that is expected to be generated through business activities over a given period of time.

Certified Public Account (CPA)

A CPA is someone who has passed a CPA accounting exam and met the government-mandated work and educational requirements to be considered a CPA.

Cost of Goods Sold (COGS)

The direct expense involved in producing the goods sold by a company. This may include the raw materials, and amount of employee labor used for production.

Credit (CR)

An accounting entry when there is either a decrease in assets, or increase liabilities and equity on the balance sheet.

Debit (DR)

An accounting entry when there is either an increase in assets, or a decrease in liabilities on the balance sheet.

Expenses (Fixed, Variable, Accrued, Operation) = (FE, VE, AE, OE)

The fixed, variable, accrued, or day-to-day expenses that a business incurs through its operation.

Generally Accepted Accounting Principles (GAAP)

These are a set of rules and guidelines that were developed by the accounting industry for companies to follow when reporting financial data.

General Ledger (GL)

A complete record of the financial transactions of a company over its lifespan.

Liabilities (Current & Long-Term) = (CL & TL)

The debts and financial obligations of a company. Current liabilities are those due to be paid within one year, whereas long-term liabilities are typically payable over a longer period of time – such as a bank loan.

Net Income (NI)

The total net earnings of a company. This is calculated by subtracting all expenses from the total revenue.

Owner's Equity (OE)

This is typically explained as the percentage amount of ownership a person has in a company. To calculate as a dollar figure, it is the remaining figure after all liabilities are subtracted from all assets.

Present Value (PV)

The value of how much a future sum of money is worth today. The value of money will change over time due to inflation, so $100 today is not worth the same amount as $100 in 10-years time. Present value helps us to understand this.

Profit & Loss (P&L)

A financial statement that is used to summarize the performance of a company over a given period of time. It summarizes all revenues, costs, and expenses that a company incurs over a period of time.

Return on Investment (ROI)

A measurement of how much of a return that a company made from a particular investment. It is calculated by dividing the net profit by the cost of the investment. It is often presented as percentage figure.

Conclusion

Thanks again for taking the time to read this book!

Hopefully you now have a greater understanding of accounting, and the importance of it in your business.

If you enjoyed this book, please take the time to leave me a review on Amazon. I appreciate your honest feedback, and it really helps me to continue producing high quality books.

65544440R00038

Made in the USA
Middletown, DE
28 February 2018